ALLEN SMITH

Memorizing the Story of Abraham and the Sacrifice Isaac

Memorize Scripture, Memorize the Bible, and Seal God's Word in Your Heart

First published by Nelaco Press 2021

Copyright © 2021 by Allen Smith

All rights reserved. No part of this publication may be reproduced, stored or transmitted in any form or by any means, electronic, mechanical, photocopying, recording, scanning, or otherwise without written permission from the publisher. It is illegal to copy this book, post it to a website, or distribute it by any other means without permission.

Scripture quotations are from The ESV® Bible (The Holy Bible, English Standard Version®), copyright © 2001 by Crossway, a publishing ministry of Good News Publishers. Used by permission. All rights reserved.

First edition

ISBN: 978-1-952381-76-8

This book was professionally typeset on Reedsy.
Find out more at reedsy.com

To my Lord and Savior

Contents

Before You Begin	1
Introduction	2
How To Use This Book	4
Week 1 Prep Work	6
Genesis 22:1	9
Genesis 22:2	11
Genesis 22:3	13
Genesis 22:4	15
Genesis 22:5	17
Genesis 22:6	19
Week 2 Prep Work	22
Genesis 22:7	24
Genesis 22:8	26
Genesis 22:9	28
Genesis 22:10	30
Genesis 22:11	32
Genesis 22:12	34
Week 3 Prep Work	36
Genesis 22:13	38
Genesis 22:14	40
Genesis 22:15	42
Genesis 22:16	44
Genesis 22:17	46
Genesis 22:18	48
Genesis 22:19	50
Conclusion	52

Before You Begin

Hey reader, before you begin memorizing scripture, I wanted to say thank you by offering a free gift.

I wrote a book called Memorize the Sermon on the Mount and I'd like to give you a free copy.

Simply text BIBLE to (678) 506-7543 and I'll send you a free copy straight to your inbox.

I've even thrown in a free bonus gift just for you.

I pray it becomes a blessing to you as you seal God's Word in your heart.

Introduction

I would like to start off by saying that I have prayed for you, whoever you are, wherever you are, as you are just beginning to start this journey to memorize a piece of the Bible.

In this book, you're going to memorize the story about Abraham and the sacrifice of Isaac from the book of Genesis. The story shows the incredible faith of Abraham and his love for God even at the request of the life of his beloved Isaac. This story also foreshadows the eventual sacrifice of Jesus on the cross as God's only begotten Son.

At 19 verses, it will take some work on your part to commit the passage to memory.

This is a game of repetition over time and this book will guide you every step of the way.

That said, there are no tricks, magic strategies, or brain hacks to make it work.

It just takes work but work that is incredibly rewarding.

But even with all that said, there are probably excuses piling up in your head.

Little lies telling you a thousand reasons why you can't possibly remember a

INTRODUCTION

section of the Bible.

"I have a bad memory."

"I don't have enough time."

And many other reasons why you might tell yourself this won't work.

Memorizing a passage of the Bible can feel daunting but you don't need to start off by memorizing everything at once.

You just need to start with one verse.

And with that, you're ready to head to the next chapter to learn how to use this book.

How To Use This Book

By now you are probably curious how this book will work so I will quickly give you an overview.

This book covers the entire story about Abraham and the sacrifice of Isaac in the book of Genesis, English Standard Version.

This passage of scripture is broken down verse by verse and I recommend you memorize one verse each day working your way through memorizing the entire passage.

Each verse has one dedicated chapter and as mentioned before, this book uses the ESV (English Standard Version) translation. You will be guided to either repeat or recite a verse or verses during each chapter.

This book is set up so that you don't need to have your Bible in front of you to read from.

There are a handful of chapters, though optional, that are the weekly preparation chapters involving some optional prep work. This prep work will make memorizing the entire passage significantly easier and time well spent on your journey to memorizing God's Word. I highly recommend you do it, but feel free to skip it.

Also, I do not require you to say the verse number when memorizing scripture. The original scriptures were not numbered into verses so I don't believe that is a critical piece to remember. However, if you would like to state the verse number when reciting each verse, you are more than welcome to.

As you work your way through memorizing each verse, there will be days where you will get frustrated. It will seem the verse just won't stick. That is completely normal. Some verses will be significantly harder to memorize than others. That is okay. Don't be afraid to repeat a chapter if you feel you didn't quite memorize the verse that day.

If the first round of repetition didn't help it stick, the second or third round should surely do the trick.

You are ready to begin on a wonderful, spirit-filled journey to solidifying a piece of God's Word inside of your heart.

May it be an incredible blessing on your life and your personal walk with Christ.

Week 1 Prep Work

Welcome to the preparation work on your journey to memorizing a piece of scripture focusing on the incredible faithfulness of Abraham.

Like I mentioned in the introduction, this work is completely optional, but I cannot encourage you enough to do the prep work.

If you had four hours to chop down a tree with a dull axe, you would be better off sharpening your axe for two of those four hours before getting started.

This prep work is sharpening your axe.

It will make everything moving forward significantly easier.

Though it will take time, this will be time well spent which you may not realize until you begin memorizing each verse one by one.

To complete the prep work, you will need to read the passage out loud 50 times.

Sounds daunting, doesn't it?

Reading out loud Abraham and Isaac would take almost 5 minutes. Do that 50 times and you are looking at roughly 4 hours worth of reading out loud.

WEEK 1 PREP WORK

Not many people would have the luxury in spare time to squeeze that in and I'm not asking you to.

Instead of doing the entire passage in one go, you are going to do a smaller chunk that would allow you to accomplish the task in an hour or less.

You are going to focus on just the first six verses as you read them out loud 50 times.

Don't have an hour?

Do it for 30 minutes running through them 25 times.

Or commit to what you can. I assure you, whatever you do here will help.

Whenever you try to memorize something from scratch, it can feel like there is a lot of resistance to get the material to stick in your brain.

But if you are very familiar with whatever you are trying to commit to memory, it is like globbing memory glue on it before you get started.

After each week, you will have an opportunity to attempt the next block of 6 verses for the following week.

If you have decided to do the prep work, get ready to read the following chunk of verses out loud. Oh, and grab a glass of water. Your mouth can get pretty dry doing this prep work.

Please note, I left the verse numbers in the passage on the following page for your reference only.

When you are ready, begin.

MEMORIZING THE STORY OF ABRAHAM AND THE SACRIFICE ISAAC

1 After these things God tested Abraham and said to him, "Abraham!" And he said, "Here I am." 2 He said, "Take your son, your only son Isaac, whom you love, and go to the land of Moriah, and offer him there as a burnt offering on one of the mountains of which I shall tell you." 3 So Abraham rose early in the morning, saddled his donkey, and took two of his young men with him, and his son Isaac. And he cut the wood for the burnt offering and arose and went to the place of which God had told him. 4 On the third day Abraham lifted up his eyes and saw the place from afar. 5 Then Abraham said to his young men, "Stay here with the donkey; I and the boy will go over there and worship and come again to you." 6 And Abraham took the wood of the burnt offering and laid it on Isaac his son. And he took in his hand the fire and the knife. So they went both of them together. (Genesis 22:1-6 ESV)

See you tomorrow!

Genesis 22:1

Today you are going to memorize Genesis 22:1.

You are going to memorize the verse by using the 10-10-10 method.

To use this method, each verse will be repeated out loud 10 times and then immediately recited 10 times from memory. In later chapters, you'll start combining verses and reciting those 10 times as well.

Don't worry if that was a little confusing to follow. Just follow the instructions and you will do just fine.

I understand 10 times may seem excessive and tedious, but trust me, this is necessary. There will be times where it may take you speaking a verse 5 times or more just to fully nail it down before being able to recite it from memory.

As a last word of advice before you begin, I wanted to share with you a few tips that have helped me memorize scripture:

1. Speaking the verse with conviction or emotion as you repeat or recite it from memory.
2. Emphasizing a different word each time you say it out loud.
3. Use hand motions as you speak.
4. Creating images in your head corresponding to each piece of a verse.

5. Singing a verse or a piece of a verse instead of speaking it.

Yes, you heard that last one right. It's weird, it works, but don't feel you need to incorporate all of these at once or any at all. As you go deeper into memorizing scripture, you will find what works for you and what doesn't.

Let's begin.

Say the following verse out loud ten times. You do not have to say the citation within the parenthesis.

"After these things God tested Abraham and said to him, 'Abraham!' And he said, 'Here I am'" (Genesis 22:1).

When you are done, recite the verse ten times in a row from memory, doing your best not to look at the verse.

Great job! You got your first verse down!

Throughout your day when you are driving your car, taking a break from work, or cooking a meal, go over what you've memorized so far to keep reinforcing it in your mind.

Tomorrow you'll quickly review what you learned today and add another verse to it.

If you don't feel confident you've truly memorized today's verse, consider going through the chapter again.

See you tomorrow!

God Bless.

Genesis 22:2

Today you are going to memorize Genesis 22:2.

After you review what you have already learned, you are going to memorize today's verse using the 10-10-10 Method.

Let's begin.

Let's review the verse you learned yesterday by reciting it 10 times from memory. Glance over it if you need a refresher.

"After these things God tested Abraham and said to him, 'Abraham!' And he said, 'Here I am'" (Genesis 22:1).

When your review is done, let's get into today's verse.

Say the following verse out loud 10 times.

"He said, 'Take your son, your only son Isaac, whom you love, and go to the land of Moriah, and offer him there as a burnt offering on one of the mountains of which I shall tell you'" (Genesis 22:2).

When you are done, recite the verse 10 times in a row from memory, doing your best not to look at the verse.

MEMORIZING THE STORY OF ABRAHAM AND THE SACRIFICE ISAAC

Great job! You got your next verse down!

You know the drill. Throughout your day when you're driving to work, taking a break from work, or cooking a meal, go over what you've memorized so far to keep reinforcing it in your mind.

Tomorrow you'll quickly review what you learned today and add another verse to it.

If you don't feel confident you've truly memorized today's verse, consider listening through the chapter again.

See you tomorrow!

Good Bless

Genesis 22:3

Today you are going to memorize Genesis 22:3.

After you review what you have already learned, you are going to memorize today's verse using the 10-10-10 Method.

Let's begin.

Let's review the verse you learned yesterday by reciting it 10 times from memory. Glance over it if you need a refresher.

"He said, 'Take your son, your only son Isaac, whom you love, and go to the land of Moriah, and offer him there as a burnt offering on one of the mountains of which I shall tell you'" (Genesis 22:2).

Now you're going to review all the verses you have memorized up to this point by reciting them 10 times. You can find it in the prep work chapter for this week if you need a refresher. If after three times you feel confident in your ability to recite all the verses you have currently memorized, feel free to call it good enough.

When your review is done, let's get into today's verse.

Say the following verse out loud 10 times:

"**So Abraham rose early in the morning, saddled his donkey, and took two of his young men with him, and his son Isaac. And he cut the wood for the burnt offering and arose and went to the place of which God had told him**" (**Genesis 22:3**).

When you are done, recite the verse 10 times in a row from memory, doing your best not to look at the verse.

Great job! You got your next verse down!

You know the drill, throughout your day when you're driving to work, taking a break from work, or cooking a meal, go over what you've memorized so far to keep reinforcing it in your mind.

Tomorrow you'll quickly review what you learned today and add another verse to it.

If you don't feel confident you've truly memorized today's verse, consider listening through the chapter again.

See you tomorrow!

God bless.

Genesis 22:4

Today you are going to memorize Genesis 22:4.

After you review what you have already learned, you are going to memorize today's verse using the 10-10-10 Method.

Let's begin.

Let's review the verse you learned yesterday by reciting it 10 times from memory. Glance over it if you need a refresher.

"So Abraham rose early in the morning, saddled his donkey, and took two of his young men with him, and his son Isaac. And he cut the wood for the burnt offering and arose and went to the place of which God had told him" (Genesis 22:3).

Now you're going to review all the verses you have memorized up to this point by reciting them 10 times. You can find it in the prep work chapter for this week if you need a refresher. If after three times you feel confident in your ability to recite all the verses you have currently memorized, feel free to call it good enough.

When your review is done, let's get into today's verse.

MEMORIZING THE STORY OF ABRAHAM AND THE SACRIFICE ISAAC

Say the following verse out loud 10 times:

"On the third day Abraham lifted up his eyes and saw the place from afar" (Genesis 22:4).

When you are done, recite the verse 10 times in a row from memory, doing your best not to look at the verse.

Great job! You got your next verse down!

You know the drill, throughout your day when you're driving to work, taking a break from work, or cooking a meal, go over what you've memorized so far to keep reinforcing it in your mind.

Tomorrow you'll quickly review what you learned today and add another verse to it.

If you don't feel confident you've truly memorized today's verse, consider listening through the chapter again.

See you tomorrow!

Genesis 22:5

Today you are going to memorize Genesis 22:5.

After you review what you have already learned, you are going to memorize today's verse using the 10-10-10 Method.

Let's begin.

Let's review the verse you learned yesterday by reciting it 10 times from memory. Glance over it if you need a refresher.

"On the third day Abraham lifted up his eyes and saw the place from afar" (Genesis 22:4).

Now you're going to review all the verses you have memorized up to this point by reciting them 10 times. You can find it in the prep work chapter for this week if you need a refresher. If after three times you feel confident in your ability to recite all the verses you have currently memorized, feel free to call it good enough.

When your review is done, let's get into today's verse.

Say the following verse out loud 10 times:

"Then Abraham said to his young men, 'Stay here with the donkey; I and the boy will go over there and worship and come again to you'" (Genesis 22:5).

When you are done, recite the verse 10 times in a row from memory, doing your best not to look at the verse.

Great job! You got your next verse down!

You know the drill, throughout your day when you're driving to work, taking a break from work, or cooking a meal, go over what you've memorized so far to keep reinforcing it in your mind.

Tomorrow you'll quickly review what you learned today and add another verse to it.

If you don't feel confident you've truly memorized today's verse, consider listening through the chapter again.

See you tomorrow!

God bless.

Genesis 22:6

Today you are going to memorize Genesis 22:6.

After you review what you have already learned, you are going to memorize today's verse using the 10-10-10 Method.

Let's begin.

Let's review the verse you learned yesterday by reciting it 10 times from memory. Glance over it if you need a refresher.

"Then Abraham said to his young men, 'Stay here with the donkey; I and the boy will go over there and worship and come again to you'" (Genesis 22:5).

Now you're going to review all the verses you have memorized up to this point by reciting them 10 times. You can find it in the prep work chapter for this week if you need a refresher. If after three times you feel confident in your ability to recite all the verses you have currently memorized, feel free to call it good enough.

When your review is done, let's get into today's verse.

Say the following verse out loud 10 times:

"And Abraham took the wood of the burnt offering and laid it on Isaac his son. And he took in his hand the fire and the knife. So they went both of them together" (Genesis 22:6).

When you are done, recite the verse 10 times in a row from memory, doing your best not to look at the verse.

Great job! You got your next verse down and your first block of 6 verses, too!

With your first block of verses completed, I would love to hear what you think so far about the book in the form of a review.

Reviews help other listeners find this book so that they too can become more intimate with God's Word.

Better yet, leaving a review is easy.

Simply go to the book's page on Amazon, scroll down and click the 'leave a customer review' button, choose a rating, leave a few words, and you're done!

Bonus points for leaving a picture with your review.

Super bonus points for a video.

Just a few minutes of your time will help people from all over the world, people you may never meet in this life, find this book and seal God's Word in their hearts.

Tomorrow you have the optional prep work for the next block of 6 verses. Though it's not mandatory, I can't stress enough how beneficial it will be moving forward.

If you plan to skip it, simply move to the following chapter to begin memorizing the first verse of the next block of 6 verses.

See you tomorrow!

God Bless!

Week 2 Prep Work

If you are here, that tells me you are ready for your next block of verses to memorize.

Great job so far. I know it takes a lot of time and effort to memorize scripture and I hope all that time and effort has been a joyful experience.

Just like with the first round of prep work, this is completely optional.

You are not required to do this to memorize the next block of 6 verses.

But like I said before, it will make the task much easier.

If you are not up for the prep work, feel free to skip this chapter.

If you are willing to give it a shot, get ready to read the next 6 verses out loud 50 times which will take you about an hour.

If you don't have an hour, run through them 25 times which will only take you about 30 minutes.

Or commit to whatever you can.

Anything and everything you do here will help moving forward.

Please note, I left the verse numbers in the passage for your reference only.

When you are ready, begin.

7 And Isaac said to his father Abraham, "My father!" And he said, "Here I am, my son." He said, "Behold, the fire and the wood, but where is the lamb for a burnt offering?" 8 Abraham said, "God will provide for himself the lamb for a burnt offering, my son." So they went both of them together. 9 When they came to the place of which God had told him, Abraham built the altar there and laid the wood in order and bound Isaac his son and laid him on the altar, on top of the wood. 10 Then Abraham reached out his hand and took the knife to slaughter his son. 11 But the angel of the Lord called to him from heaven and said, "Abraham, Abraham!" And he said, "Here I am." 12 He said, "Do not lay your hand on the boy or do anything to him, for now I know that you fear God, seeing you have not withheld your son, your only son, from me." (Genesis 22:7-12)

See you tomorrow!

Genesis 22:7

Today you are going to memorize Genesis 22:7.

After you review what you have already learned, you are going to memorize today's verse using the 10-10-10 Method.

Let's begin.

Let's review the verse you learned last by reciting it 10 times from memory. Glance over it if you need a refresher.

"And Abraham took the wood of the burnt offering and laid it on Isaac his son. And he took in his hand the fire and the knife. So they went both of them together" (Genesis 22:6).

Now you're going to review all the verses you have memorized up to this point by reciting them 10 times. You can find it in the prep work chapter for this week if you need a refresher. If after three times you feel confident in your ability to recite all the verses you have currently memorized, feel free to call it good enough.

When your review is done, let's get into today's verse.

Say the following verse out loud 10 times:

"And Isaac said to his father Abraham, 'My father!' And he said, 'Here I am, my son.' He said, 'Behold, the fire and the wood, but where is the lamb for a burnt offering?'" (Genesis 22:7).

When you are done, recite the verse 10 times in a row from memory, doing your best not to look at the verse.

Great job! You got your next verse down!

You know the drill, throughout your day when you're driving to work, taking a break from work, or cooking a meal, go over what you've memorized so far to keep reinforcing it in your mind.

Tomorrow you'll quickly review what you learned today and add another verse to it.

If you don't feel confident you've truly memorized today's verse, consider listening through the chapter again.

See you tomorrow!

God bless.

Genesis 22:8

Today you are going to memorize Genesis 22:8.

After you review what you have already learned, you are going to memorize today's verse using the 10-10-10 Method.

Let's begin.

Let's review the verse you learned yesterday by reciting it 10 times from memory. Glance over it if you need a refresher.

"And Isaac said to his father Abraham, 'My father!' And he said, 'Here I am, my son.' He said, 'Behold, the fire and the wood, but where is the lamb for a burnt offering?'" (Genesis 22:7).

Now you're going to review all the verses you have memorized up to this point by reciting them 10 times. You can find it in the prep work chapter for this week if you need a refresher. If after three times you feel confident in your ability to recite all the verses you have currently memorized, feel free to call it good enough.

When your review is done, let's get into today's verse.

Say the following verse out loud 10 times:

"Abraham said, 'God will provide for himself the lamb for a burnt offering, my son.' So they went both of them together" (Genesis 22:8).

When you are done, recite the verse 10 times in a row from memory, doing your best not to look at the verse.

Great job! You got your next verse down!

You know the drill, throughout your day when you're driving to work, taking a break from work, or cooking a meal, go over what you've memorized so far to keep reinforcing it in your mind.

Tomorrow you'll quickly review what you learned today and add another verse to it.

If you don't feel confident you've truly memorized today's verse, consider listening through the chapter again.

See you tomorrow!

God bless.

Genesis 22:9

Today you are going to memorize Genesis 22:9.

After you review what you have already learned, you are going to memorize today's verse using the 10-10-10 Method.

Let's begin.

Let's review the verse you learned yesterday by reciting it 10 times from memory. Glance over it if you need a refresher.

"Abraham said, 'God will provide for himself the lamb for a burnt offering, my son.' So they went both of them together" (Genesis 22:8).

Now you're going to review all the verses you have memorized up to this point by reciting them 10 times. You can find it in the prep work chapter for this week if you need a refresher. If after three times you feel confident in your ability to recite all the verses you have currently memorized, feel free to call it good enough.

When your review is done, let's get into today's verse.

Say the following verse out loud 10 times:

"When they came to the place of which God had told him, Abraham built the altar there and laid the wood in order and bound Isaac his son and laid him on the altar, on top of the wood" (Genesis 22:9).

When you are done, recite the verse 10 times in a row from memory, doing your best not to look at the verse.

Great job! You got your next verse down!

You know the drill, throughout your day when you're driving to work, taking a break from work, or cooking a meal, go over what you've memorized so far to keep reinforcing it in your mind.

Tomorrow you'll quickly review what you learned today and add another verse to it.

If you don't feel confident you've truly memorized today's verse, consider listening through the chapter again.

See you tomorrow!

God bless.

Genesis 22:10

Today you are going to memorize Genesis 22:10.

After you review what you have already learned, you are going to memorize today's verse using the 10-10-10 Method.

Let's begin.

Let's review the verse you learned yesterday by reciting it 10 times from memory. Glance over it if you need a refresher.

"When they came to the place of which God had told him, Abraham built the altar there and laid the wood in order and bound Isaac his son and laid him on the altar, on top of the wood" (Genesis 22:9).

Now you're going to review all the verses you have memorized up to this point by reciting them 10 times. You can find it in the prep work chapter for this week if you need a refresher. If after three times you feel confident in your ability to recite all the verses you have currently memorized, feel free to call it good enough.

When your review is done, let's get into today's verse.

Say the following verse out loud 10 times:

"Then Abraham reached out his hand and took the knife to slaughter his son" (Genesis 22:10).

When you are done, recite the verse 10 times in a row from memory, doing your best not to look at the verse.

Great job! You got your next verse down!

You know the drill, throughout your day when you're driving to work, taking a break from work, or cooking a meal, go over what you've memorized so far to keep reinforcing it in your mind.

Tomorrow you'll quickly review what you learned today and add another verse to it.

If you don't feel confident you've truly memorized today's verse, consider listening through the chapter again.

See you tomorrow!

God bless.

Genesis 22:11

Today you are going to memorize Genesis 22:11.

After you review what you have already learned, you are going to memorize today's verse using the 10-10-10 Method.

Let's begin.

Let's review the verse you learned yesterday by reciting it 10 times from memory. Glance over it if you need a refresher.

"Then Abraham reached out his hand and took the knife to slaughter his son" (Genesis 22:10).

Now you're going to review all the verses you have memorized up to this point by reciting them 10 times. You can find it in the prep work chapter for this week if you need a refresher. If after three times you feel confident in your ability to recite all the verses you have currently memorized, feel free to call it good enough.

When your review is done, let's get into today's verse.

Say the following verse out loud 10 times:

"But the angel of the Lord called to him from heaven and said, 'Abraham, Abraham!' And he said, 'Here I am'" (Genesis 22:11).

When you are done, recite the verse 10 times in a row from memory, doing your best not to look at the verse.

Great job! You got your next verse down!

You know the drill, throughout your day when you're driving to work, taking a break from work, or cooking a meal, go over what you've memorized so far to keep reinforcing it in your mind.

Tomorrow you'll quickly review what you learned today and add another verse to it.

If you don't feel confident you've truly memorized today's verse, consider listening through the chapter again.

See you tomorrow!

God bless.

Genesis 22:12

Today you are going to memorize Genesis 22:12.

After you review what you have already learned, you are going to memorize today's verse using the 10-10-10 Method.

Let's begin.

Let's review the verse you learned yesterday by reciting it 10 times from memory. Glance over it if you need a refresher.

"But the angel of the Lord called to him from heaven and said, 'Abraham, Abraham!' And he said, 'Here I am'" (Genesis 22:11).

Now you're going to review all the verses you have memorized up to this point by reciting them 10 times. You can find it in the prep work chapter for this week if you need a refresher. If after three times you feel confident in your ability to recite all the verses you have currently memorized, feel free to call it good enough.

When your review is done, let's get into today's verse.

Say the following verse out loud 10 times:

GENESIS 22:12

"He said, 'Do not lay your hand on the boy or do anything to him, for now I know that you fear God, seeing you have not withheld your son, your only son, from me'" (Genesis 22:12).

When you are done, recite the verse 10 times in a row from memory, doing your best not to look at the verse.

Great job! You got your next verse down!

You know the drill, throughout your day when you're driving to work, taking a break from work, or cooking a meal, go over what you've memorized so far to keep reinforcing it in your mind.

Tomorrow you have the optional prep work for the last block of 7 verses. Though it's not mandatory, I can't stress enough how beneficial it will be moving forward.

If you plan to skip it, simply move to the following chapter to begin memorizing the first verse of the last block of 7 verses.

If you don't feel confident you've truly memorized today's verse, consider listening through the chapter again.

See you tomorrow!

God bless.

Week 3 Prep Work

If you are here, that tells me you are ready for your last block of verses to memorize.

Great job so far. I know it takes a lot of time and effort to memorize scripture and I hope all that time and effort has been a joyful experience.

Just like with the first round of prep work, this is completely optional.

You are not required to do this to memorize the last block of 7 verses.

But like I said before, it will make the task much easier.

If you are not up for the prep work, feel free to skip this chapter.

If you are willing to give it a shot, get ready to read the last 7 verses out loud 50 times which will take you about an hour.

If you don't have an hour, run through them 25 times which will only take you about 30 minutes.

Or commit to whatever you can.

Anything and everything you do here will help moving forward.

WEEK 3 PREP WORK

Please note, I left the verse numbers in the passage for your reference only.

When you are ready, begin.

13 And Abraham lifted up his eyes and looked, and behold, behind him was a ram, caught in a thicket by his horns. And Abraham went and took the ram and offered it up as a burnt offering instead of his son. 14 So Abraham called the name of that place, "The Lord will provide"; as it is said to this day, "On the mount of the Lord it shall be provided." 15 And the angel of the Lord called to Abraham a second time from heaven 16 and said, "By myself I have sworn, declares the Lord, because you have done this and have not withheld your son, your only son, 17 I will surely bless you, and I will surely multiply your offspring as the stars of heaven and as the sand that is on the seashore. And your offspring shall possess the gate of his enemies, 18 and in your offspring shall all the nations of the earth be blessed, because you have obeyed my voice." 19 So Abraham returned to his young men, and they arose and went together to Beersheba. And Abraham lived at Beersheba. (Genesis 22:13-19)

See you tomorrow!

Genesis 22:13

Today you are going to memorize Genesis 22:13.

After you review what you have already learned, you are going to memorize today's verse using the 10-10-10 Method.

Let's begin.

Let's review the verse you learned yesterday by reciting it 10 times from memory. Glance over it if you need a refresher.

"He said, 'Do not lay your hand on the boy or do anything to him, for now I know that you fear God, seeing you have not withheld your son, your only son, from me'" (Genesis 22:12).

Now you're going to review all the verses you have memorized up to this point by reciting them 10 times. You can find it in the prep work chapter for this week if you need a refresher. If after three times you feel confident in your ability to recite all the verses you have currently memorized, feel free to call it good enough.

When your review is done, let's get into today's verse.

Say the following verse out loud 10 times:

GENESIS 22:13

"And Abraham lifted up his eyes and looked, and behold, behind him was a ram, caught in a thicket by his horns. And Abraham went and took the ram and offered it up as a burnt offering instead of his son" (Genesis 22:13).

When you are done, recite the verse 10 times in a row from memory, doing your best not to look at the verse.

Great job! You got your next verse down!

You know the drill, throughout your day when you're driving to work, taking a break from work, or cooking a meal, go over what you've memorized so far to keep reinforcing it in your mind.

Tomorrow you'll quickly review what you learned today and add another verse to it.

If you don't feel confident you've truly memorized today's verse, consider listening through the chapter again.

See you tomorrow!

God bless!

Genesis 22:14

Today you are going to memorize Genesis 22:14.

After you review what you have already learned, you are going to memorize today's verse using the 10-10-10 Method.

Let's begin.

Let's review the verse you learned last by reciting it 10 times from memory. Glance over it if you need a refresher.

"And Abraham lifted up his eyes and looked, and behold, behind him was a ram, caught in a thicket by his horns. And Abraham went and took the ram and offered it up as a burnt offering instead of his son" (Genesis 22:13).

Now you're going to review all the verses you have memorized up to this point by reciting them 10 times. You can find it in the prep work chapter for this week if you need a refresher. If after three times you feel confident in your ability to recite all the verses you have currently memorized, feel free to call it good enough.

When your review is done, let's get into today's verse.

Say the following verse out loud 10 times:

"So Abraham called the name of that place, 'The Lord will provide'; as it is said to this day, 'On the mount of the Lord it shall be provided'" (Genesis 22:14).

When you are done, recite the verse 10 times in a row from memory, doing your best not to look at the verse.

Great job! You got your next verse down!

You know the drill, throughout your day when you're driving to work, taking a break from work, or cooking a meal, go over what you've memorized so far to keep reinforcing it in your mind.

Tomorrow you'll quickly review what you learned today and add another verse to it.

If you don't feel confident you've truly memorized today's verse, consider listening through the chapter again.

See you tomorrow!

God bless.

Genesis 22:15

Today you are going to memorize Genesis 22:15.

After you review what you have already learned, you are going to memorize today's verse using the 10-10-10 Method.

Let's begin.

Let's review the verse you learned yesterday by reciting it 10 times from memory. Glance over it if you need a refresher.

"So Abraham called the name of that place, 'The Lord will provide'; as it is said to this day, 'On the mount of the Lord it shall be provided'" (Genesis 22:14).

Now you're going to review all the verses you have memorized up to this point by reciting them 10 times. You can find it in the prep work chapter for this week if you need a refresher. If after three times you feel confident in your ability to recite all the verses you have currently memorized, feel free to call it good enough.

When your review is done, let's get into today's verse.

Say the following verse out loud 10 times:

"And the angel of the Lord called to Abraham a second time from heaven" (Genesis 22:15).

When you are done, recite the verse 10 times in a row from memory, doing your best not to look at the verse.

Great job! You got your next verse down!

You know the drill, throughout your day when you're driving to work, taking a break from work, or cooking a meal, go over what you've memorized so far to keep reinforcing it in your mind.

Tomorrow you'll quickly review what you learned today and add another verse to it.

If you don't feel confident you've truly memorized today's verse, consider listening through the chapter again.

See you tomorrow!

God bless.

Genesis 22:16

Today you are going to memorize Genesis 22:16.

After you review what you have already learned, you are going to memorize today's verse using the 10-10-10 Method.

Let's begin.

Let's review the verse you learned yesterday by reciting it 10 times from memory. Glance over it if you need a refresher.

"And the angel of the Lord called to Abraham a second time from heaven" (Genesis 22:15).

Now you're going to review all the verses you have memorized up to this point by reciting them 10 times. You can find it in the prep work chapter for this week if you need a refresher. If after three times you feel confident in your ability to recite all the verses you have currently memorized, feel free to call it good enough.

When your review is done, let's get into today's verse.

Say the following verse out loud 10 times:

"And said, 'By myself I have sworn, declares the Lord, because you have done this and have not withheld your son, your only son'" (Genesis 22:16).

When you are done, recite the verse 10 times in a row from memory, doing your best not to look at the verse.

Great job! You got your next verse down!

You know the drill, throughout your day when you're driving to work, taking a break from work, or cooking a meal, go over what you've memorized so far to keep reinforcing it in your mind.

Tomorrow you'll quickly review what you learned today and add another verse to it.

If you don't feel confident you've truly memorized today's verse, consider listening through the chapter again.

See you tomorrow!

God bless.

Genesis 22:17

Today you are going to memorize Genesis 22:17.

After you review what you have already learned, you are going to memorize today's verse using the 10-10-10 Method.

Let's begin.

Let's review the verse you learned yesterday by reciting it 10 times from memory. Glance over it if you need a refresher.

"And said, 'By myself I have sworn, declares the Lord, because you have done this and have not withheld your son, your only son'" (Genesis 22:16).

Now you're going to review all the verses you have memorized up to this point by reciting them 10 times. You can find it in the prep work chapter for this week if you need a refresher. If after three times you feel confident in your ability to recite all the verses you have currently memorized, feel free to call it good enough.

When your review is done, let's get into today's verse.

Say the following verse out loud 10 times:

"'I will surely bless you, and I will surely multiply your offspring as the stars of heaven and as the sand that is on the seashore. And your offspring shall possess the gate of his enemies'" (Genesis 22:17).

When you are done, recite the verse 10 times in a row from memory, doing your best not to look at the verse.

Great job! You got your next verse down!

You know the drill, throughout your day when you're driving to work, taking a break from work, or cooking a meal, go over what you've memorized so far to keep reinforcing it in your mind.

Tomorrow you'll quickly review what you learned today and add another verse to it.

If you don't feel confident you've truly memorized today's verse, consider listening through the chapter again.

See you tomorrow!

God bless.

Genesis 22:18

Today you are going to memorize Genesis 22:18.

After you review what you have already learned, you are going to memorize today's verse using the 10-10-10 Method.

Let's begin.

Let's review the verse you learned yesterday by reciting it 10 times from memory. Glance over it if you need a refresher.

"'I will surely bless you, and I will surely multiply your offspring as the stars of heaven and as the sand that is on the seashore. And your offspring shall possess the gate of his enemies'" (Genesis 22:17).

Now you're going to review all the verses you have memorized up to this point by reciting them 10 times. You can find it in the prep work chapter for this week if you need a refresher. If after three times you feel confident in your ability to recite all the verses you have currently memorized, feel free to call it good enough.

When your review is done, let's get into today's verse.

Say the following verse out loud 10 times:

"'And in your offspring shall all the nations of the earth be blessed, because you have obeyed my voice'" (Genesis 22:18).

When you are done, recite the verse 10 times in a row from memory, doing your best not to look at the verse.

Great job! You got your next verse down!

You know the drill, throughout your day when you're driving to work, taking a break from work, or cooking a meal, go over what you've memorized so far to keep reinforcing it in your mind.

Tomorrow you'll quickly review what you learned today and add another verse to it.

If you don't feel confident you've truly memorized today's verse, consider listening through the chapter again.

See you tomorrow!

God bless.

Genesis 22:19

Today you are going to memorize Genesis 22:19.

After you review what you have already learned, you are going to memorize today's verse using the 10-10-10 Method.

Let's begin.

Let's review the verse you learned yesterday by reciting it 10 times from memory. Glance over it if you need a refresher.

"'And in your offspring shall all the nations of the earth be blessed, because you have obeyed my voice'" (Genesis 22:18).

Now you're going to review all the verses you have memorized up to this point by reciting them 10 times. You can find it in the prep work chapter for this week if you need a refresher. If after three times you feel confident in your ability to recite all the verses you have currently memorized, feel free to call it good enough.

When your review is done, let's get into today's verse.

Say the following verse out loud 10 times:

"So Abraham returned to his young men, and they arose and went together to Beersheba. And Abraham lived at Beersheba" (Genesis 22:19).

When you are done, recite the verse 10 times in a row from memory, doing your best not to look at the verse.

Great job! You got your last verse down!

You know the drill, throughout your day when you're driving to work, taking a break from work, or cooking a meal, go over what you've memorized so far to keep reinforcing it in your mind.

If you don't feel confident you've truly memorized today's verse, consider listening through the chapter again.

God bless.

Conclusion

If you are here, I hope that means you have fully memorized the story about Abraham and the sacrifice of Isaac from the book of Genesis.

I hope the experience was rewarding and enriching as you sealed part of God's Word in your heart.

I recommend reciting the full passage every day for the next 30 days to truly solidify that piece of scripture in your mind.

Once you're done, consider memorizing another passage or even an entire book of the Bible!

Lastly, if you have enjoyed this book, do consider leaving a review. I look forward to seeing your feedback.

May God bless you on your journey to further know Him, and I leave you with these two verses, "All Scripture is breathed out by God and profitable for teaching, for reproof, for correction, and for training in righteousness, that the man of God may be complete, equipped for every good work" (2 Timothy 3:16-17).

www.ingramcontent.com/pod-product-compliance
Lightning Source LLC
Chambersburg PA
CBHW030139100526
44592CB00011B/967